Tiger Upstairs
on Connecticut Avenue

Books and chapbooks by Elisavietta Ritchie

Feathers, Or, Love on the Wing (2012)
From the Artist's Deathbed (2012)
Cormorant Beyond the Compost (2011)
Real Toads (2008)
Awaiting Permission to Land (2006)
The Spirit of the Walrus (2005)
In Haste I Write You This Note: Stories (2000)
The Arc of the Storm (1998)
Elegy for the Other Woman (1996)
Flying Time: Stories & Half-Stories (1992, 1996)
Wild Garlic: Journal of Maria X. (novella in verse, 1995)
A Wound-Up Cat & Other Bedtime Stories (1993)
The Problem with Eden (1985)
Raking the Snow (1982)
Moving to Larger Quarters (1977)
A Sheath of Dreams & Other Games (1976)
Tightening the Circle Over Eel Country (1974)
Timbot (novella in verse, 1970)

Poetry anthologies edited
Finding the Name (1983)
The Dolphin's Arc: Poems on Endangered Marine Species (1986)
Here, Even the Blue Crabs Create (2009)

Tiger Upstairs
on Connecticut Avenue

Elisavietta Ritchie

Cherry Grove Collections

Published by Cherry Grove Collections
P.O. Box 541106
Cincinnati, OH 45254-1106

ISBN: 9781625490292
LCCN: 2013940869

Poetry Editor: Kevin Walzer
Business Editor: Lori Jareo

Visit us on the web at www.cherry-grove.com

Author website: www.elisaviettaandclyde.com

Special thanks to those who have given me advice and encourage-
ment on individual poems and on the whole collection, in particular:
Jorge Artamonoff, Jaye Chantal, Leslie Dickey, Rocky Jones, Ann
Brewer Knox, Cliff Lynn, Helena Mann-Melnichenko, Howard Ro-
man, Carol Russell, Suzanne Shelden, Donald Shomette, Susan Sonde,
Elisabeth Stevens, Martin Tucker, and my fellow members of the
Washington Writers' Publishing House who have likewise long pro-
vided inspiration, expertise, and friendship.

Above all, I thank my chief muse and editor, Clyde Henri Farnsworth.

Certain of the aforementioned are no longer around to thank.

Dedicated to
Clyde Henri Farnsworth

Acknowledgments

We thank the editors of the various publications where most of the poems in this collection saw print, some in earlier versions:

"A Different Jungle Story": *Lalitamba*, Nov. 2013;

"Amadeo Modigliani: *Adrienne (Woman with Bangs)*": *The Broadkill Review*, Vol. 6, No, 1; *From the Artist's Deathbed, The Winterhawk Press Anthology of Chapbooks*, 2012;

"Another Poet Diagnosed": *Loch Raven Review*, 2013;

"Another Side to the Coin": *Earth's Daughters*, issue 81, *Both Sides Now*, 2012;

"Auguste Renoir: *Lady with a Parasol in a Garden*": *The Broadkill Review*, Vol. 6, No, 1; *From the Artist's Deathbed*;

"Begging the Dead," *Visions International*, # 86, 2012; *From the Artist's Deathbed*;

"Camille Pissarro's *Artist's Garden at Eragny*": *The Broadkill Review*, Vol. 6, No, 1; *From the Artist's Deathbed*;

"Camille Pissarro: *The Bather* Speaks": *The Ledge*, winner The Poetry Prize, 2012; *From the Artist's Deathbed; The Art of Survival: an anthology*, Kings Estate Press, in-press, editor Ruth Moon Kempher, 2014;

"Can't You Tell I'm Working?" *The Broadkill Review*, 2009;

"Frontier Station": *Poetry Now*, Vol. 2, No. 4; *Feathers, Or, Love on the Wing*, Shelden Studios 2012;

"The Gypsy is Summoned Before the Commandant," *Whose Woods These Are; Finding The Name*, Wineberry Press, 1983; *From the Artist's Deathbed*;

"Io and I": *The Ledge*, 2000;

"Kingfisher on My Bookcase," *Visions International*, Nov. 2011; *From the Artist's Deathbed*;

"Learning Shorin-Ryu on Eighty's Thin Edge": *The Broadkill Review*, Vol. 6, No. 4;

"Lobster, Conanicut Island, Narragansett Bay" as "For a Certain Artist": *Folio* 2000; *Potomac Review*, 2000;

"My Father, Colonel, U.S. Army, Retired," *NewCollage*, Fall 1978;

I.

Neighbors Speak Their Minds About That Lady Up the Street

She falls in love with all she meets, the fool—
Can't choose among a daisy, rose, or weed
but crams them all in one bouquet
in a crystal vase or old coke can—
                              Invites
workmen in muddy boots, tramps, diplomats
from countries nowhere on *our* globes, *artistes,*
rat-loving scientists in velvet jeans—
Trotsky's grandniece and a Russian prince
at her same dining table? Where's her tact?

Picks up some hitchhiker who spent the night
in jail— *mistake,* he swears, it's cold and far
and no one else has given him a ride,
got miles to walk till he gets home again.
She invites him for a meal!
                              Hangs out with
tattooed bikers, bouncers, mavericks, cranks.
What mess of accents, shades and origins,
traveling zoos and dynasties of strays,
storm- tossed squirrels, lost cats, orphan ducks, strange
men—
                Who knows what lot she sleeps with?
Or sleeps not?

Punching, kicking, tangling at karate—
Give us propriety, decorum, please!

13

Camille Pissarro: *The Bather* speaks

I must have been quite beautiful back then,
am still surprised how many men pursued…

I let them think me but a starchy prude
until we paddled up the river when
the day was fair, light yellow, blue and green.

I was afraid the sun would leave
freckles on my breasts and we'd conceive
an unexpected child from where we'd been
cavorting in the shallows by the bank
of tiger lilies, peppermint and moss—

We yearned for more, but foliage was dank
with spilled champagne and sticky with cassis.

A need to pee, then nettle stings, kept me
from further loss of maidenhood …

Each loss is the first, and never quite the same.
Those early days, I never understood.

I have made many famous but forget their
                                        names,
dear artists who would sketch me in the nude.

I was a willing model: French plumbing then
                                        was crude.

So they would scrub me till I shone, then came
to hang on this renown museum wall,
my loveliness immortalized in paint.

Although my grandmothers would faint,
I have no regrets I gave to art my all.

Search Parties

I am out with lanterns,
searching for myself.
-Emily Dickinson

For me, a candle should suffice.
Barring that—a match.
No lamp that burns too bright
Or lasts—

Self, no angel,
Disappoints, stuns—
Mirrors yield danger,
Leave us wrung,

Are more honest?
In mirrors a flame
Deceives, reflects,
Flickers blame.

Truth no spice cake
Love is crumbs-
In walls, mice wait
alert, not dumb—

Night Watchman

That night I slept all night in your arms
and all night you did not sleep, what did
you see while you peered through my skull?

Did I veil myself in a scrim of dreams?
Did you unravel them one by one,
braid together those banners of silk
to create a magic quilt for our bed?

Or did you discover it less gossamer
inside this round bone, caverns dark,
close as a mine whose dangerous shafts
collapsed as you passed, lantern on cap?

Did you count layers of lovers inside,
some with whom I never did sleep,
friendly sardines in the tin of my mind…

I hope you made the most of your chance
to explore the terraced landscape within.

I lack a map through my labyrinth.

Please draw me a topographical chart,
highlight any shifts of tectonic plates,
plot us a road through that risky terrain.

August Renoir: *Lady with Parasol in a Garden*

I slip through the flowering crowds,
avoid bees schooling around me.
A parasol shades my face from the sun,
from their stingers, their trickster eyes.

My petticoats skim peony beds,
other beds where I've slept
or not slept or still might—
who is to know?

I glide through this garden as if
through a novel-in-progress,
an observer-scribe,
imagine, perceive, take notes—

Like a spider, long-legged, Latin name longer*,
I pause near azaleas, inspect a neglected web,
weigh which fly, gnat or small arachnid to nab,
let my mandibles crunch, then devour at dusk.

Pholous phalangiodes

Why I Have Not

One button gone, your shirt
is more intriguing, leaves you
unguarded, even flawed.

Questions arise: how was it lost?
Now we have a plot—love
story, mystery, possibly noir—

a chance to describe not just
the shirt but the wearer
as well as that Other who
can't or won't wield a needle.

In certain Far Eastern cultures
perfection affronts the Almighty
Who only is perfect.

Therefore a batik-maker is glad of an odd
dab of wax on her fabric,
a painter leaves one corner blank,

not ignoring the gap, but still
aware of his own imperfection,
the need to strive higher.

The impudence of it. Bless
the leopard with irregular spots,
the asymmetrical ocelot,

and the house cat, that creature
considered nearest perfection
but less a threat to the gods

if a tattered ear, crooked tail,
whiskers missing... I cannot find thread
or needle to stitch you beyond perfection.

Soft Spots for a deaf Siamese cat

I heard her purrs. She could not, or our
learned conversations above her head, she
a skinny princess fallen on hard times,

> Siamese, like the destitute prince my
> father rescued in a blizzard, student
> searching for a flop house in an odd
> district in Chicago. Sent to study in
> America, his funds soon ran out. My
> father brought him home to a couch
> shared with our angora tabby, King
> Tutankhamen, who warmed him all
> Christmas week—I kept that couch
> years, for other strangers and cats.

Today my hosts push her off her chair so
I can sit there, though I demur. This act
requires my offer of lap and a caressing.

> In Greek the word for *stranger* and *guest*
> the same: *ksenos*. Did my Russian émigré
> father tell his stranger/guest how once *he*
> trudged snowy battlefields seeking safety,
> reached Ellis Island midwinter penniless,
> slogged through storms on a New Haven
> campus, shoveled coal, tutored calculus,
> French and Russian to pay for his meals?

I warm her elderly feline bones, don't
murmur baby talk she can't hear, or
mind beige hairs on new black slacks.

> Fifty years passed. My father's job took him
> to Bangkok. The prince, doing well, greeted
> him warmly. Both preferred tropical climes,
> kept cats, and shared incipient hearing problems.
> My father was merely related to princes.

My hosts offer to rent me their deaf
Siamese cat. I will take her any time,
I too rescue strays lost in a blizzard.

Tiger Upstairs
on Connecticut Avenue
For Taj, at Tai Chi

"He is crouching here, pat him."

We swirl our intricate patterns
over invisible white-tufted ears.

Any feline leaps at fluttering hands
for his diversion and ours, aware
fingers aren't genuine butterflies.

> *My mind flutters back to orange-and*
> *-brown butterflies clustered on mud*
> *by the jungle river in Taman Negara.*
>
> *Nights, a Malay tiger encircled our hut,*
> *might have leapt through windows not*
> *screened, shutters imperfectly hinged,*
>
> *One swipe of his paw could rip*
> *the mosquito netting over our bunks—*
>
> *Every morning we found tiger prints.*

Our palms stroke air, aware this tiger
could snatch our fingers, five at a bite.

Taj switches venues. "Imagine
we're now in a cell, fire in the pit,
a pot of water is boiling, vapor—"

"Where's the tiger?" I ask.
"Forget the tiger," he says.

You can't just dismiss a tiger.

The tiger *is* here, in the steam,
grooms orange-black-white fur,
cleans his whiskers, claws, teeth.

He tips the pot. The water cools.
His tongue furls to a funnel, laps—
Belly-up, he rolls in the puddle.

> *Tigers don't mind being wet:*
> *one paddled behind our raft*
> *as we poled that brown river.*

Hard to focus on ritual patterns,
a tiger patrolling the premises.

> *I recall that envoy from Okinawa*
> *nabbed as a spy in China, thrown*
> *in a cell with a tiger unfed a week.*

> *Guards peered through the bars stunned*
> *to observe their captive perform Tai Chi*
> *while the tiger watched, soon fell asleep.*

The prisoner shared rations of rice and tea
with the beast, practiced his martial dances.

At week's end they released him. His tiger?

Your tiger trails me down the stairs
to the avenue, the whole way home,
leaves prints on my Ningxia carpet,
orange-and-black hairs on my bed.

You, Similarly Feline

Lion cub
In my lap
Cote d'Ivoire 1976

Purrs locomotive
Rough tongue
Swabs my cheeks

Furry paws
Curl
Knead my thighs

But in a flash
Claws
Could stretch

"Pain—"

Tai Chi, Herb Garden, October

What did Taj say?
His words slid into space
while breeze from our arms
stirred furry-tipped sage.

Ennoblement,
that's the gist,
pain liberates—

Liberates limbs
from their sockets?

Frees broken toes
to break off, crumble
among the cilantro?

Thigh muscles to knot
like jungle vines?

In coldest winters
rosemary won't wither
will vibrate fragrance
over the heedless snows.

Pain *thinks,* ergo *exists,*
longer than thyme
or these valiant
and holey bones.

Learning Shorin-Ryu
on Eighty's Thin Edge

Garlic, ginger, peppers, soy sauce, fried rice,
raw fish, strip steaks and sweat—scents waft
across oceans, years, indoors where I watch
virtual Internet fights, see bare feet strike bare
boards, try to imprint intricate martial arts
on my not-yet-waning brain...

>   *Two decades ago in Toronto, I practiced*
>   *Japanese Gojo Ryu, a decade later, here,*
>   *fell oddly ill, lost power to walk, or fight.*
>   *Bare feet cannot walk bare wooden floors.*

Half Okinawan, half Black Panther, our new
sensei, forty-five, spins in royal *kata* while he
lectures on karate history.

"The *sensei* who taught me was eighty-one,
we *katakan* watched in awe as he shuffled in
our *dojo*, bowed, leapt, smashed boards open-
handed, and felled all his assailants in turn."

>   *Our sensei can't know my age. I never filled*
>   *that blank when I joined our Maryland gym.*

Now I untangle my purpled limbs, swing legs
to strike shins as high as my limp kicks reach,
flick imagined sand at four unseen assailants,

whirl into unfamiliar Okinawan *kata*, mix up
neihanchi and *pinan shodan*, can't recall when
to raise both fists high, block low, *shuto* slice,
punch left, double-punch, block right, squat.

Should a *real* mob of *real* thugs on a *real* street
some dark night jump me, at least I can warn:

"You guys plan to rob me, mug, bump me off?

"I'll pounce samurai-style to crunch your
                                                    vitals,
peel your Adam's apples, bust your teeth, find
the Swiss Army knife deep in my purse, stab
your guts. After our dust-up, I will go online,
inform the world how I whipped your butts.

"You still wanna fight? Where d'you all go?"

Domenico Veneziano:
Madonna and Child

That sweet baby's gonna
give his innocent mama
a tentful of trouble.

The glint in his eyes,
twist of his lips,
predict a mischief maker

who will tip over tables,
stay too late with his elders,
hang out with riffraff.

The Mother's long smooth hands
show a lover of culture
and spiritual matters.

Not stubby fingers of an artist
who messes with charcoal and paint
or patterns rocks in the yard —

She will waste time
dreaming notable futures
for the whole family.

What peculiar guests
she entertains: those wings!
Not the typical carpenter's wife.

She may not find time to take
her twig broom to the sawdust Joe leaves,
or properly diaper the Infant.

Let's observe how
she raises that Child.
As for those halos of gold?

Both have auburn hair
and you know what they say
about redheads—watch out!

Plaint of Rattus norvegicus, Alpha Rat in Laboratory Research into Safety and Effectiveness of Forteo to Counteract Calcium Deficiencies

You pumped-up nerds who don't know
        Squeak—

My calcium level is high enough, thanks to what
the janitor sneaks into my cage: cheese, cake crumbs,
yogurt bars, unfinished cartons of ice cream, left
from your lunches, *here*, in our research lab…

You claim this squirrel wheel strengthens bones—
Boring! Can't get anywhere. Born here, I fear and
crave your world outside…   Install wide-screen TV,
stream in Tchaikovsky, no more Pop. A classical rat
weaned on Rimsky-Korsakov, I've chewed through
        scores.

Aristocratic lineage, fur sable, skin delicate,
it hurts when you shoot me up,
mainline your risky chemicals into my thighs.
We rats hate needle jabs. "Mere bee stings,
pin pricks," you say. No! Scimitars to me!
And nobody asked my permission.

My outsized bones keep growing super-strong.
Tonight I'll lift the roof of my jail, slip out.
My claws spring your locks. Rat incisors gnaw
through wooden cabinets. I see fine in the dark,
know where you hide your snacks, smokes,
                                illegal *stuff*.

Through this wire mesh, I spy a big white box. Pastry!
I sniff…Someone's birthday cake! And this is *my* birthday
too! Our lives brief, we rats celebrate each month.
At dusk you'll leave to drink your wine, spawn or
however humans do it, such low birth rates. I'll wriggle
out, snag my slice of cake, snatch the Gaga rodent in
the next cage…While the janitor cleans up, we'll slip out.

This sacra-sorca-whatever you induced erodes my
skeleton. Yet in what time left in your torture lab,
I'm MegaRat, R-Atlas, Tyrannosaurus Rat! I'll bite
the hand that shoots me next, and I carry Plague.

Yet we male rats only want to cuddle,
be laid back,
be laid.

II.

Pablo Picasso: *The Tragedy*

is knowing this is
the beach between

sea with no boat
shore with no house

the lost cannot
be remade

night is chill
feet bare, clothes thin

the child's fingers too delicate
to seize what might be

and behind the bluff
dogs strain on their chains

Childe Hassan: *Allies Day, 1917*
Veterans' Day 11/11/11

So many flags. So many
crosses. Clichés
of patriotism spin
silver cobwebs up
the poles to our skulls.

Give us this day
our daily flag.
Let us wave it at others
as they would wave at us
a thousand hands,

ghost hands thrust up
through the grass
of our far-flung graves.
Wrap me in the stars,
the stripes on their backs—

Frontier Station

Birds ignore borders
overfly all maps' lines
as lightly as song

We wait behind barriers and signs
burdened, documented
inventing our reasons

Awaiting our orders
ignoring all seasons
we keep our places

Birds keep their seasons
leave and return
whiten the barricades

Wings graze our grayed faces

The Gypsy Is Summoned
Before the Commandant

Your questions I don't understand
but in the word "interrogation" I hear
terror...I know no names.

In the past, those who questioned me
wanted only facts, histories, and names.
I know nothing about anyone till he asks.

Then I see through skin and skull,
trace seines of lines and lives...and lies.
I never forget a hand...I know no names.

I hold the sperm of half of Europe in my
                                   womb.
My Gypsy babies steal across the earth.
I know no names.

I have deciphered death in every palm.
I fear the gleam of your instruments.
I know no names.

Look, I am old. My skirts are dank
from your jail. My silver tarnished,
you stole my gold.

Yet my hair remains dark, my leg slim,
I still shake a fine tambourine.
could show you a good time.

Come, dismiss those surly guards at the gates.
Tear up your reports. Beyond these walls
my caravan awaits us both.

I could reveal the future of your regime.
I'd read your own fortune free.
Come along...I can tell you now:

The lines on my palm
are longer than yours.
And I know your name.

Aunt Maria Leonidovna Tells Me Her War Stories at Afternoon Tea

Pesochniye, a village beyond Leningrad, 1986

Two lumps, now you have brought sugar?

...Yes, dear, I wanted children
but an operation...So I adopted
an orphaned cousin...In the Siege
she died of starvation...

... Lake Ladoga a highway of ice,
the Nazis knew we were transporting
Leningrad's children by sleighs—
they strafed, shelled and bombed.

Inside Leningrad, bombs we preferred:
loud whistle while dropping gave
people time to hide, and for me
to man my gun post on the roof.

Shells hit without warning—
Sudden strike: Someone fell at our feet.
We learned to step over corpses.
No burials until spring when
at last the ground thawed...

What good all my medals for courage?
For survival. You take them home.

Do have another cup while the samovar—

My Father, Colonel,
U.S. Army, Retired
(George Artamonoff, 1902-1984)

The shell explodes and scatters light
and alien finger bones. He isn't sure
if this is real or dream
but screams until he wakes.

The household wakens also, terrified.
He is embarrassed, and confused,
trapped back at Kharkov, Sebastopol, Anzio,
Monte Cassino, Normandy, Battle of the Bulge.

Forty years have passed, the wars have not.
Shrapnel, rubble and peculiar shards of flesh
still litter all the bedroom floor so deep
he cannot find his slippers in the dark.

Communiqués from an Émigré

1.
Have we faded from each other's lives the way
sepia photographs fade, and people in wars
lose each other? Our fathers, second cousins,
lost contact through several wars…

2.
You were nine in Occupied Belgium when
without warning SS soldiers snatched
your class of blond blue-eyed sons
of Old Russian exiles,
locked you onto an eastbound train to grow up
Germans, become future janissaries.

They made you goosestep Berlin streets, salute their
swastikas, sing *Deutschland Uber Alles*,
aim a wooden rifle,
sort their wounded sent home from the Front.

Allied planes hit their targets, rations sparse,
you learned to scavenge the ruins of Cologne.

In Brussels, your parents mourned
their kidnapped child.
Your mother descended from Nicholas I
(by-product of his love for the court artist's daughter,
noble yet not royal enough
to become a tsarina, a tsar must marry
a full-blooded princess, albeit imported).

Do royalty, legitimacy, bereavement, matter
to soldiers, bare cupboards, soup kitchens?
One carries on.

3.
World War Two over, your father, now head
of a UN refugee camp, retrieved you.
My father still in Europe located yours,
and helped you all launch new lives in Brazil.

Did you relearn a childhood in peace?
You studied Portuguese, English, engineering and
Buddhism, prospered, married, spoke seldom of the war,
and not to your children...

4.
We met in warm South Atlantic surf. *Distingué*
as a prince, you resembled my dashing father.

The same books lined your shelves as on mine,
our children born the same years as if siblings.
We both had suitable spouses.
Neither remained forever.

5.
Your rare visit north, you held my hand
on the busy street—normal in Latin lands,
but in America then reserved
for sweethearts, genuine fiancés.
We never became bona fide lovers, alas.
Still, you left footprints on my poems...

6.
Thirty years later, hemispheres apart,
we began to write every day,
emailed on the Internet, shared
histories, secrets, quotidian details, first drafts.

Like twins or lovers, we thought the same thoughts
the same moment, learned we cooked the same meals,
suffered similar ailments, each cared for a damaged son.
Ancestral ghosts wandered into both our lives without
notice.
Your forbearers had fallen in love with third cousins.

At last your letters described
your dangerous childhood in Europe,
showed me how to survive, how to live.
Dangers persist, wait to catch us off guard…

7.
Without warning you have cut the connection,
our daily tryst in the stratosphere. No news,
no obit, no one down there thinks to write, or knows
where. To whom could I write?
For whom? Silenced, I mourn, cannot believe you died
without first telling me.

8.
Today I learn: *you are alive!*
So, we will both die old, far apart
but, perhaps, both on the same night…

A Different Jungle Story

We'll walk this jungle
forever! No parents goad.
Only captors.

We never dared touch,
are now bound together: ropes
lash our ankles, wrists.

At least they untied
our blindfolds,
we can see—

We see trees, stumble
on banyans, grab saplings
to scale muddy slopes—

Trickster Jacob's Ladders
lead to another ridge, down
to another ravine.

Leaves mottle the sky.
Sunlight filters down. Night
turns phosphorescent:

old logs become patches
of moonlight, worms gleam green,
sparks zip up the night.

Who knows we're missing
from somewhere? Have we crossed
borders? No customs.

Part of a war which
moves without shadow or tracks,
(dawns we see tiger prints),

forced to trudge on, we
don't know where we are going,
where we have been.

We slip on wet leaves. They
yank us into monsoons.
But rain, we can drink!

Trails disappear in logs
logs bridge a stream. If I
slip, we both fall.

All swim thick rivers.
All bleed from leeches, blood
crimson as ginger blooms.

I place one ginger
bloom in your fingers. No sign
you notice, recall—

Eloquent once, now
always mute. Their blow to your
head knocked out speech.

You are not
wholly amnesic: in streams
you seem to pray.

They slap me to silence.
Who could overhear—rainbowed birds,
monkeys, millipedes?

Guards whisper. No tongue
I decipher. In mine, they
know commands, and oaths.

We lose weight daily.
Yet guards share bananas, rice,
dried fish and chilies.

They roast a squirrel,
gnaw bones clean. We eat in
silence, watched by rifles.

I watch you. Before
across tables our eyes held
brave conversations

mouths dared not speak. Now
between us are vines, toadstools,
orange butterflies, mud.

At least they keep us
leashed like two hounds, six
feet of rope between us.

I hide a moment
beyond a banyan, you
pretend not to see.

You don't. They broke your
glasses, maybe your mind. They
aren't sentimental—

unlike your friends who
schemed we be alone in that
hut where they brought us:

"Collect fishermen's
tales, will take days..." We followed
figures flowing, tide

down the beach, till they
vanished. Did your friends also
arrange the ambush?

Do they cover our
absence with their inventions?
Your friends protect you.

Foreign and fair, I
appeared. "Destined," they said, and
want you to have me.

Our captors may know
your importance. For barter?
Might I have some worth?

May not be clear who
we are. Papers were taken,
who knows where, to whom.

Towns in the hills burned
to the ground. Jungle
devours old camps.

We lose traces, traits,
move like migrating creatures.
What value to them?

You don't know I'm here.
But at night, curled like beasts in
a cave or lean-to,

guards watch as we move
close for warmth—nights, jungles blow
cold—you curl around.

Bound, hands still caress,
bound, legs can encircle and we
become conjoined twins.

This dawn your lips are
moths on my ear: *Keep playing*
the game. Understand

our freedom: danger
is not here in the jungle.
We break camp, march on.

Outside the Jailhouse, a sequence

1.
Fledglings, June

En route to the Courthouse, I hesitate

Is another rescue possible, worth it
or should we leave things and wings
and him alone…?

On the parapet bounding outside stairs
high above the wet parking lot
a starling, new, fuzz unkempt,
squawks and squawks

So far to fall

I have vertigo too, understand
the orphan condition, should
carry him inside for crumbs

But the motel-room lock
has clicked behind me
I'm already late for court

And now know: *I must go*

2.
Hot Wind, Long Avenues

Alone I walk
toward the courthouse
Long lines inside

One empty seat
The need to wait
Must find ID

In my bag one postcard
left from yesterday's
museum: Edvard Munch
Gescgerei (The Scream)

That scream beyond
small boats distant
in the Nordic fjord
beyond distracted passersby
uninterested in why

My scream now
silent here outside
Visitation Room
City Jail

I forgot photo ID
driver's license
Unidentifiable
without documents

impotent, unknowable
potentially dangerous
to inmates and guards
I can't go inside

Gone my chance
to speak by remote TV
with a manic son
off his meds

got in a fight
lost to cops
they locked him up

Outside the Visitation Room
the wooden bench
is hard on bones
fresh gray paint
wafts and clings

Sheriff's chair inside
has cushioned seats
His revolver real
My son had none
Same barber buzzed
both heads

A lady with blond wool hair
and gleaming chocolate skin
comes out to offer sympathies
glad to sit out here

Her younger son also
locked up, he be home
in June, praise the Lord

She talked with him
(the son, the Lord)
Grandkids turn now
to use that intercom

Her other son
a Correction Officer
she knows they keep it
winter-cold inside

He'll need you to deposit cash
for thermals and a snack
You feed bills in that red box
It wants only twenties and
the guards take three bucks out

What do I know
of the system, the law
of heights and depths
of another's pain

I only know
we both must try
to set things right

All the while
in this Southern port
small distant boats

involved in their
own lines and seines
sail in their spheres

and passersby
down the quay
pay no heed
to any scream

3.
Courtroom Sketchbook

Daumier might have drawn the rutabaga-faces
above floppy collars or waistcoats,
high-buttoned boots, spats.
One black robe.

Daumier would have sketched
these skinny prisoners fed peanut-buttered white bread
stale at four a.m.,
caught their lock-step shuffles in split sandals,
chains thrice-looped around
striped pajamas gray-on-gray,
caught their lowered heads, their glances
toward a judge rotund and righteous as a god,
(not one of those wondrous naughty gods on Mount
Olympus).

What artist could record their fears?

This unartistic day, we strain to catch
the judge's admonitions.
The case has not been closed.
The trial is etched in us.

4.
Across the Green

Must wait at a station where
no train has yet to stop, or pass,

wind belies the heat on tracks,
sections mashed as if a giant sledge
had hammered home.

I lack tools to lay new tracks,
await a parolee who may, may not,
be sprung today, hand-cuffs, leg-cuffs, chains
unlocked, gray-striped pajamas shed.

Or he might not see the sun for months
only filtered through the bars

or moon or waves or boats—

I have been there,
will wait here.

5.
Sunday, September

Today he and his children played
on a distant beach. His voice overflowed
the phone. "They buried themselves
in the sand, swam in the surf—"

I, more tuned to these hours, this decade,
in an unorchestrated silence
not entirely beyond
beaches, curses, prayers, or tears of relief,
what to do from here but rejoice

until it happens again.

6.
Osmosis

Your dreams slip through iron bars,
filter through lead,

float over oceans,
ride hurricanes,

find me in the desert,
curl round like a mist,

slip in through my pores,
re-form in my head

New Life Rag

a stranger's kitchen cutlery
a rollaway with broken springs
locked cupboards with another's things

each night I wake (nights when I sleep)
dry-mouthed yet find upon my tongue
like dust the taste of borrowed rum

Again That Toad

The gray-beige toad
can climb a screen!

He falls…Although
no outlet at the top

his four fat fingers
hoist his mottled weight

up, up the mesh
once more, once more.

III.

Richard Chew: *Lobster*
Conanicut Island, Narragansett Bay

We sailed your twenty-foot boat,
crimson as passion is meant to be,
beached her between strata of slate,
built a driftwood fire, filled the pail.

While we waited for sea water to heat
you sketched the lobster, combative
as models are not meant to be.

Then you plunged him headfirst
into our boiling sea, swore he died
too fast to feel pain. When he turned
scarlet, we cracked claws with stones,
pried carapace with your marlin spike.

We feasted while you told me how Braque
used fifty-nine different colors
(I'd labeled his paintings somber),
Picasso sketched on café tablecloths,
Cezanne never finished a work.

At eighteen you were already bound
for the Art Students League in New York.

Because we both dripped lobster juice
and the sea was now dark, we skinny-swam
all the way to the farthest buoy.

Out came the full moon. Beached on sand,
you turned your back. "Hurry," you urged.
"Get dressed before you catch cold!"

We shoved off, sailed home, sat on
the boatshed roof, only talked.

At the door of the cottage my mother rented,
your lips grazed my cheek. That kiss entered
a poem, my first to see print. I was sixteen.

For Christmas you sent me your favorite '78s:
Tristan and Isolde: "Love Duet,"
Forza del Destino, "Overture."
Also your canvas fragrant with oil:
our lobster, green and live on the ocean floor.

In a Soho gallery a decade later I discovered
my portrait you sketched that night
in your moonlight mind, later painted in oils. Too
expensive to buy.

Lobster remains bluegreen on my wall.

Amadeo Modigliani: *Adrienne (Woman with Bangs)*

I study the artist who
celebrates my extended neck,
slit onyx eyes,
and cassis-red lips.

My nose is a ski jump,
hands pale orange lumps,
my sideburns too dark
and should be clipped.

Yet I get away with murder—
he calls my almond eyes
the eyes of an icon, or lion.
They do know how to look.

He steals out my door...
I spy through the panes
as he fills in his sketch
au Café des Espoirs Perdus.

He dips his pen unaware
in his cassis, sweetens the lips
as he sweetened mine
with dark-cherry kisses and wine.

Camille Pissarro: *Artist's Garden at Eragny:* The Artist's Wife Speaks

How can I get back to sleep
this warm April night?

He woke me up to complain
he cannot sleep at all.

In fact he's been snorting and snuffling
all night like a boar after truffles

while I was dreaming in colors
what plants we should buy.

Awake, I recall: *no francs for flowers
until he sells a painting.* His oils are all wet.

I steal into the night. Full moon
shows patches his dog dug bare

while *he* was stretching his costly *toiles*
and daubing paint on his models.

My apron pockets hide seeds,
bulbs sprout in my drawers.

I plant larkspur, peonies, hollyhocks,
zinnias, marigolds for their ruffled suns.

At eight he awakes. *"Regardes, ma cherie!*
While we slept, blossoms leapt from my
                                    palette!

But where is my *café au lait*?
And we cannot eat posies for supper."

To survive through next winter
I plant rutabagas, potatoes and leeks,

scrub mud from my fingers,
sprinkles, nightshade on his vichyssoise.

Can't You Tell I'm Working?

I can't say that. He wants to talk.
He could have seen my fingers tap.
He *needs* to chat so I can't hide, or flip.

Must smile, inquire, "You'd like some tea?"
Up to me to tweak the stove.
"Water's cold, takes time to heat…"

"Good time for conversation then,
good time to eat another meal."
He's pleased with his creative time today.

I've not half used up mine—sixteen personae
on the loose, in limbo caught, destinies
unsolved—If I pause they'll slip away—

"Did you pay this bill?" "Not due this week."
"Where are my pills?" "There, in your paints."
"And what's for lunch?" "No time, no francs."

I clean my spectacles with vigor, crack
one lens. My parched notebooks thirst
for words, my brain leaks paragraphs.

Outsiders think me cheerful, kind. I don't
shirk scrubbing his paint-splattered shirts,
the cooking pots he burnt. I darn his socks.

So I can't be unseemly, scream,
Leave me alone, my love,
for God's sake, let me also work!

Henri de Toulouse Lautrec: *At the Café: The Customer and the Anemic Cashier, Who Complains*

None of my suitors interest me
for a long-term alliance, and those
who *are* interesting don't suit—

too old or too young, too fat or too thin,
one lacks a job, another loves only his work.
All love the absinthe I pour.

Those who intrigue me already have
wives with more money than I
and their claws scratch.

I prefer men who beguile me with chocolates,
champagne and wondrous tales,
but they spin on and on, would love me
all night while *I* need my sleep:

must unlock the café at dawn, mop the floors,
count yesterday's cash,
and splash on more perfume
before my next dalliance—

IV.

Kingfisher on the Bookshelf

1.
Not my house, not sure whose, this a dream,
but I *saw* a flicker up there—No, *Kingfisher*!

Last autumn I freed one from the gazebo:
Crested, iridescent, black-blue, hatpin eyes.

This bird hunches among stacked books.
I reach up, cup my hands over the wings.

Should have considered those
needle claws, ice-pick beak.

At a door I release him, then worry: a nest
among all those books? Abandoned chicks?

2.
"If you don't write for days," you ask,
"do undone poems emerge as dreams?"

Like feathers, should I gather dreams,
risk blood-letting beaks, open doors?

My kingfisher an omen?
Lone birds could be.

Conundrums

To pick a chip
of ice from tiles
don't hold a second
in your fingers

deep wisdom here
yet Chinese say
to catch a horse
must ride a horse

what if they both
gallop away
leave you dangling
from your saddle

you sprawl in mud
and slip on ice
your rides have fled
so in the end

not horse nor ice
can be retrieved
you drink warm tea
then learn to walk

Prompters

Even before I've conceived the thoughts
silent words somewhere beyond my ears
trigger my fingers to write.

My dramatis personae meanwhile, full-blown,
idle my precious time away in the stratosphere,
on call in the wings, awaiting cues
for me to snarl, unsnarl, resnarl their problems.

If someone or something interrupts,
if I don't cast a net and haul them in quickly,
they will drift off like smoke.

I must settle their squabbles, petty dilemmas,
hear out their grand illicit affairs.

As if I could sort out and solve all my own
amid the fragrance of ash.

Pierre Bonnard: *The Letter*
At Deadline

Had we but reams of time
to fill 5000 pages with our love

turn clocks upside down
reset two pairs of hands

clasps would snap inside
chronometers, springs uncoil—

what timeless tomes
we would create—

Another Side to the Coin

"...no poetry in money..." Billy Collins

Yet look at *these* coins
flung like words on the bar
each in its tiny puddle
corona of froth
how they intoxicate—

dimes in the depths
of washer and drain
eloquent, inaccessible—

exotic coins lively with loons,
beavers, emus and roos,
minted to outlast
thousands of hands—

stately with profiles
of antique deities
and silvery queens
plump and proud
to hold a job
heads not yet off

always another side
to their stories...

Hear the rhythms of rupees,
clink of crowns,
flipping of francs,

language of lira,
patter of pesos,
ding of dong—

Dance with dinars,
sniff Malaysian ringets—
turmeric, curry—
yearn for yen—

And consider two pennies
far from humble
these gleam like truth
from the street, the pool,
the eyes of the dead—

Lines Composed at MeiWah Restaurant Ten Minutes Before A Poetry Reading For Which I'd Overlooked My Bag of Books

1.
Before my first book
appeared in print
a plane flew me west
to a mountain side where
I was Slated to Read.

I climbed the trail.
Campfires lighted the slope.
Throngs gathered to hear me.
Major Literary Lions
prowled the heights.

Unbuckling my pack,
I realized: *my manuscript
remained on the plane...*

Always rewriting, I don't
memorize my work.
And in the smoky glow
I stood utterly naked.

In those days people said
I was pretty. Still I was not
inclined to strip for free.

Somehow I carried it off.
A dream, you say, *of great
psychological import?*

2.
What relief when the publisher
printed my book! At last
I could hold my head high,
keep my clothes on.

For my bookless reading tonight,
what is the drill?

Stag Crashes Writers' Workshop

1.
The stag with a rack of a dozen points
stalks down our driveway again,
leaps the stream into our jungle-yard,
jumps in our neighbors' flowerbeds
to our delight and their pique.

While we prune adverbs, the stag prunes
azaleas, scatters our pages, thoughts—

The poets assembled exclaim, "Remember
Stafford's doe struck in the night—"

"He shoved her over the mountainside—"

"A fawn in her belly—"

"Then drove home to scribble his famous—"

"*Infamous* poem—"

2.
I'd have delivered that fawn Caesarian-style
(Swiss Army knife in my fanny pack),
bundled him in my coat, nursed
with a baby bottle, repaired my fence,
though hard to housebreak, raised as a pet."

3.
Since every poet must someday describe a deer
alive, dying, or dead, all settle down to write...

4.
The antlers catch on a laurel bush.
He strides off, chomps his way through
everyone's gardens,
then wanders through the ravine,
 well-fed laureate but a shifty muse.

Archetypal Affairs:
Romance Writing 101

1.
The Plot with Obstacles
Any romance has conflicts: your characters must have
plenty, and know their great love
is doomed:

They've met late in life, on a steamer or train,
romantic enough in whatever setting,
and in transit means fleeting.
Could be she is older, or he too much so,
or they live far apart, come of rival clans,
and jealous spouses have prior claims
and sixth senses.

This won't stop the protagonists
from "falling in love"
in the requisite lightning flash.

2.
The Progression
Just as well then they exchange only glances
at alien tables, touch in passing
as if by accident.

Had situations been other, they might have found
a deserted meadow, beach, any flat ground,

or tumbled into a peony patch

blessedly clear of bees,
a warm sea without jellyfish.
Or a feather bed, and for longer?

3.
Admonition
Don't let your heroine age, grow ugly, nurse sextuplets
unless each has a different sire
à la Madame de Stael and writes best-sellers.

And you can't kill off your hero or heroine!
Mishaps need but *seem* life-threatening.

4.
In Conclusion
Since this framework is archetypal,
you as writer must fill in the setting,
invent what banal details I omit.

And we know how affairs evolve.
Most end in a swamp.

Edouard Manet:
La Gare Saint-Lazare
The Lady Speaks

I wait for the train
with the black locomotive
that wears a bouquet
of phlox in the window.

I am tired of waiting
every day at the station,
so is your daughter
and so is your dog.

If you don't arrive by tonight,
I will buy tickets
to Cannes for the winter.
In Cannes, there are other men.

When at last you arrive from Marseilles
you will find the flat bare
but for one strand of dark
auburn hair, a blue satin bow.

Yet if you arrived with bouquets
of tulips, despite your usual excuses,
I'd prepare *rognons de veau*
and bake a *torte aux cerises*.

I've forgiven others who came
hungry and tired and late.
One turned up with daisies
at four a.m. That one, him I wed.

But oh, this terrible smoke
and noise of the trains!
How long must we wait?
How long this time will you stay?

I Wander, Lonely

Skinny fingers
of clouds
like robot limbs
stretch to snatch
wisps of words
until they too
dissolve in blue

or hang forlorn
as my dress
on a branch
by a stream when
I'm in without

My connections
pending retrieval
oogle each other
tweet through the galaxy

One missile strike
or keystroke
would delete
everything
OMG
no way to access
Facebook or salvation

And all my links unhook themselves
while I Google u

My One-Tree Cherry Orchard

Mine sprang by surprise from a lover's seed
spit over the balcony rail. During all
my journeys, the sapling became a tree:
white blossoms, maroon fruit, shiny trunk, tall.

Cherry trees poetic, row after row,
my lone tree strews petals, then the fruit hits
and litters the deck and flagstones below.
My spouse calls my grand tree his nemesis,

complains he must sweep, then threatens to
                                        chop.
Never! I hide the axe. Cherries fall, squish,
paint an original Jackson Pollock
on our deck. Pits reach the stream, feed
                                        crawfish.

Who was it who inadvertently sowed
that long-ago seed? Which of my sweethearts?
Good thing that particular lover flowed
on: fruit like BBs, ephemeral, tart.

My husband chops that tree. But from the base
new twigs sneak out in time to shade my face.

Shopping Expedition

Her husband smiled, *"Ton portrait est si bon!"*
Then as he left, hung it in the *salon.*

A note from her would-be love, avant-garde
artist X: *"I stopped to leave you my card,*
saw your portrait young—Comme tu étais belle!
Our paths crossed too late… I totalement fell—"

She writes back what both know, don't speak,
                              don't dare:
"We would have had a cyclonic affair,
made babies and art…Life gave us no chance…"
She sighs, cries, and savors their missed
                              romance.

She needs brushes and bras (hers old as she):
while the carriage drives her to Monoprix
she wipes her tears and considers her list…
Paint brushes aren't cheap, like silk in her fist.
Lingerie is confusing, frightfully dear…

Ah! black lace two-for-one: her choice is clear.
She unwraps one ample black-lace brassiere,
pulls up black stockings, a spiderweb pair,
dons a carmine camisole though this dye
is made from crushed beetles, females who die.

To *café au lait* with her artist love—

Must dodge his fake halo that floats above
his head...He's back from some duty-free isle
where it's too hot and bras are not in style.

Her lover's herpetological bent
unnerves her, but now her beauty is spent
she'll ignore his paint and turpentine smell
and hope that afterwards no one can tell.

Black lace worked years ago with quite a few...
Relieved his eyesight has now gone askew,
before she crosses that grim River Styx
she sets out for one more quick caffeine fix—

The Scholars, Emeritus

Bodies no longer svelte, by day
they are sleek in the latest styles
of a couple of decades ago,

nights they favor long shirts
and gowns though they miss
bare skin on bare skin.

They may confuse villanelles and sestinas,
sonnets and stocks, students who look alike
with odd electronic appendages beeping.

New England winters become much too cold,
they mull over Siena, Venice, Madrid,
but getting there is no more half the fun,

They fret about flash points in the Med,
the African incontinent—He lectured on
Bardic traditions in deserts and jungles,

she lobbied against circumcision, wrote op-ed
pieces on various Rights, marched for Causes,
so they might be unwelcome in certain lands.

While they fret if olives or prunes in the fridge
she doles out his pills, he massages her feet,
and they weigh living wills.

O (Ablative) To Be Reborn
a Cellist—

to my doppelganger

Even curled inside my cage of flesh,
his fetal fist would grasp a fan of bows
strung with tails of stallions fresh
from Olympus, set to perform, compose.

Each note, a black balloon stuck to a pole,
would tremble, leap up from the page
and soar like wedge-tailed eagles on a roll,
my locomotive love not yet assuaged.

He would arrive equipped with novel tones.
His spruce-and-maple instrument
full of air would echo with the groans
of godlike passion never spent.

He'd learn new symphonies at but one glance,
and even on his wet-winged natal day
he'd trigger oceans full of whales to dance,
oaks to waltz, rocks sing, mountains sway—

V.

Updating the Address List

Delete all the dead?
Banish from the screen—

they hide in arcane folds
of the stratosphere,

crouch on clouds,
peer down, wave,

mock our attempts
to scrub their existence,

refuse deletion,
persist.

Another Poet Diagnosed
for Hilary Tham,
who had just emailed me her news

1.
What is it about our chests and breasts?
Hearts too full spill secrets, lines on palms
reveal more truths than those we write.

Others analyzed our sonnets, villanelles,
judged our work worthy, or not.
Now they critique our cells and blood.

Poets already take a bad enough rap
for skewing national suicide rates.
No! We struggle like thistles to survive.

Why must we, who would *bring* light,
face the dark like everyone else?
Aren't poets supposed immortal?

We were put on earth not only to praise it
or show off our would-be bohemian lives
of sin and song. *A writer's task,* said Camus,

is to speak for the silenced, imprisoned
in their souls or lives or literal jails.
Why silence us in the face of so much need?

2.
This week Doctor Warren probes
my questionable left breast,
presses points of pain, not as tried

that awkward boy with auburn hair,
(both 15, we skimmed forbidden manuals
but did not reach the final chapter).

Doctor Warren, ace seismologist, tests
my ominous fault zones, dangerous magma
that churns deep inside volcanoes,

while I lie back, count syllables in my head,
smooth meters and memorize rhymes before
my hard-drive brain crashes, chest explodes.

Doctor Warren offers *me* hope for the moment.
Yet bards can grow forgetful with age, the most
lyrical flesh dissolves like a poem in a puddle.

So we cling to strands of ink, our webs of form
and content are spider trampolines stretched
between orange tiger lilies and salmon
                                    hibiscus.

These bloom for a day then, overnight, their
flamboyant garb shrivels, and like old poets,
petal by petal they drop, and, usefully, rot.

Midnight Mass, St. Nicholas,
Easter 2011

Though the owl hoots from the woods all night
(merely love-sick calls for a mate?)
and vultures wheel overhead all day,

thus far alive, with the faults
and cares of the living,
I squeeze inside heavy doors
through the crowd,
light candles to swarthy saints
who gaze with disdain
on the Easter throngs,
and wait through the endless chants
for the midnight blessing that never quite
blesses but hangs us all,

and pay my annual visit to ghosts who float under
the dome. Must cherish them all,
but pray for and try to tend to the living.

Luncheon Parties

The dying come to lunch on my balcony.
We pick up conversations from last week/
month/year as if the Black Serpent had not
wound himself into an obsidian wreath,
the owls not called across their yards.

You, for instance, have told me how few weeks
(days) your doctor promised you –*how can
he guess?* Next-of-kin aren't always informed,
don't want to believe bad news. *You* do know,
share predictions with me. We weigh omens.

My benign Black Rat Snake stays curled
in my neglected orchard, *my* owl flew,
to wit-to-woooos in the neighbors' garden.
You've launched your books, paid your bills,
tidied archives and kitchen. *I* don't clean my
                                          desk.

Now you knock on my door, early as ever, take
your usual chair, admire the enameled locket you once
brought me, the blooming cherry tree
this sprang up by surprise—wasn't it you, who
flicked a cherry pit over the balcony long ago?

I've again prepared your favorite filet of sole,
you bring your beloved Folinari Pinot Grigio,
extract the cork, pour but not to your normal
level in the glass, then recork the bottle, place
this in my fridge, and do not finish your plate.

We resume our tête-à-tête: *Explain, not so fast,*
dark matter — You know I'd have eloped with you —
We agreed to disagree on politics — I still think you short-
sighted/misguided/pigheaded, my sweet!
Won't you have more Camembert, Concord grapes?

We converse, not without effort maintain
                                        repartee,
denounce double negatives and eschew clichés,
don't mention vacation plans, new manuscripts
or the season's schedules of operas and plays.
Next week's obits inform: that visit was your
                                        last.

Answering Service

His message drifts
from my voice mail

No time to talk
Scant time alone

Soon they'll return
His whispers fade

How his words rang
our secret years

His body now
consumes itself

They have explained
how it will end

They reassure
he won't feel pain

He slips away
I pull him back

I knew how brief
our days to love

He knew how brief
our years to live

Begging the Dead

Evenings we meet—
same street, same café.
Ever discreet, dead

lover, dead spy, you
still travel light.
I'll accept a ghost.

Cold coffee, stale rolls,
untouched wine:
my turn to pay.

You know this world,
time to explore
unknown realms.

Wait—
I unfurl new drafts,
await your words,

then,
in silence,
go.

On Assignations: Total Recall

"Again we run into each other here!"
a new friend exclaims. "As if we
had arranged assignations! So—"
Polite, I smile.

I'm catapulted to old assignations with *you*—
at street corners, corner cafes, our wide bridge.

How amazing we two should meet, by accident or
                                        by chance
on the same street, same bridge, same hour, day
                                        after day.

No accident. A chance.
Our luck no one noticed.

Now a narrower, bridge stretches between us,
spans a ravine into which neither would
                                        choose to fall.

You already have… And yet if by now
our unabridged luck has not worn out

when *I* cross, taking care to avoid the edges,
by chance you will be waiting at the far end.

Whatthehell then
if anyone spies.

Medical Offices, Halloween Week

1.
A skull of papier maché glows in a plastic nest
at knee-level beside your receptionist's desk.

Orange bunting, pumpkins, red-orange leaves,
all artificial, festoon the room and they mean

to cheer us. Yet, how many trick-or-treat nights
remain? Who will see the Christmastree lights?

2.
You speak of your father dying painfully long,
bonds between daughters and fathers
                                especially strong.

I still mourn mine, though he died Aprils ago,
                                confess
I damn those who labeled his death: *a blessing*.

3.
Some nights, if not fully, my father returns:
my sensible stepmother wanted him burned,

so his bountiful heart and encyclopedic mind
dissolved in the flames. Not a bone can I find.

Unlike Saint Jerome, I have no skull to address.
No saints, Daddy or I, but we caused no
                                distress.

4.

Beyond rescue, our fathers now ash, dust or
                                        cinders,
we must cherish the living. How many more
                                        winters?

From unholy sockets, that skull's ruby eyes
like gumdrops wink-wink their seasonal lies.

VI.

Skirting the Hot Wires

Fallen across the street
they blocked the way.
The storm did a job.

We must dodge
what might kill us
or else confront it.

I can't wrest heavy
magnolia limbs
thrust in the mud

but free three short
branches, strip
ragged leaves,

fill the crystal vase
though my swollen wrist
is broken or sprained.

Tree-toppling storms
and pain remind: like
magnolia and wires,

though damaged, tangled,
we mostly stand straight,
alive and dangerous still.

A thick branch crashes
two seconds after I walk
under the dead locust tree.

Seminal Questions: *Raisons d'être*

"Meditate upon one seminal question,"
Taj says while we stretch. "Not ask
whether: *After Qi Gong, Coffee or Tea?*
or *What is My Purpose in This Universe?*

"But some point that begs your attention.
You may not find answers. The question
might be enough…"

          Already my mind
snaps up his jettisoned questions the way
a turtle's jaws lock on chunks of tomato
cut out where green hornworms invaded.

What *is* my purpose here in our world?
Should abandon any idea I could fix it:

not skilled enough to mend a Machina,
not rich enough to set everything right
with a pen to a check, or brash enough
to create more Commandments— this
was tried once before, who heeds all Ten?

Slav enough to use that word *soul,* and
I *have* connected one soul with another…

Can't save my own—those mighty
Commandments like redwood trees
cast their shade over the blooming
sunflower fields of my colorful life.

We float in this limited space, weigh
coffee later—No, green tea is better.

Could my mission distill to this: nourish
stray cats, stray children, strayed lovers;
create, connect, delete words all of which
will soon dissolve in puddles or clouds.

A handicapped Dea Ex Machina, at last
clear I must keep on *doing/not doing*, try
to repair what machines I can, and *live*.

Io and I

So I brought her home,
Zeus' reluctant gift, rib-thin,
mud-caked, whimpering,

a runt not guaranteed to live,
not worth a farmer's care,
would never fetch a price.

No cow in our pastures
would accept the waif:
each has her own dark calf.

At home, her welcome was uneven.
"It will eat so much!" "A horse
would make more sense—"

"Where would you keep the beast?"
"The potting shed is small, paved
with stones, veiled with spider webs."

I washed her down with rosemary
until, like ivory, she gleamed,
and wreathed her in jasmine vines,

then lined a corner of my room
with geraniums, poured milk into a flask.
She sucked it dry, and slept.

Soon the children fought for rides.
The gardener, grateful for her dung,
liked how she cropped the grass.

But her mournful moos disturbed us all,
her rapid growth created problems,
she sullied and got into everything.

The garden was well fenced with thorns—
she forced a gap, ate melons, pears,
lettuce, and ransacked the vineyard.

She disdained the droughty pond,
stuck her nose in silver bowls,
tried to join the table like a guest.

She snatched shawls off the line,
draped herself in linen sheets
to hide her nakedness and keep

peacocks and persistent flies at bay.
People laughed at her regalia –
she fled to the grove of oaks.

I led her home, chased flies
and peacocks off. Then I heard bellowing,
caught men beating her

for misdemeanors normal
for a heifer. I was furious when
neighbors blamed me for her scars.

In my absence, men tied her to
an oak, laid a fire, rigged
a spit, honed their blades.

I seized a knife, cut the rope,
slashed the startled men—
they squealed like swine.

Freed, she galloped to the river.
I rushed after –No sign of her,
no bovine prints in sand.

One young woman, ankle-deep,
stood scrubbing her bruised skin,
salting up the water with her tears.

I inquired if she had spied an errant cow.
She tossed her head, dove in the waves.
Lightning split the sky, hail pelted like wasps.

A Snake Disappearing: *for Oscar,*
the Black Snake at My Birthday Party

"A snake disappearing is often more memorable than one
completely visible...
Disappearance enlivens, and the vanishing is often the
form we embrace."
Mark Irwin, *The Writer's Chronicle,*
Vol. 43, No. 3.

No, disappearance saddens. You vanished.
No wake, no trace of skin or scale or bent
grass bent to reveal where you slithered.

That was your presence I embraced.

All muscle and anthracite gleam in the May
sunshine we sought together, you did not
mind when I lifted you coil by coil,
a rope tarred black for a pirate's yacht.

I let you weave around my neck,
wind upward into an Athenian wreath
for a head bystanders would call foolhardy,
the risk too great for my bravado.

One child and I traded you back and forth,
an onyx choker: guests screamed, edged
toward the grill, into the house—

We named you Oscar. So I know you.

You wintered overhead in our attic we
reach only by a ladder too steep to scale.

You found secret apertures to steal
through these century-old walls,
explore the house we *had* thought ours,
inspect paintings you left askew or else
shattered in apparent disapproval.

Then you hid on the broom closet shelves
with bug sprays, unopened silver polish.
That June 29, my birthday, you dangled
the slippery gift of yourself.

Those of us who know our serpents
admired the sheen of your latest skin,
cut of your jaws, your hat-pin eyes.

I released you in the yard where you
keep down moles, toads, field mice,
and, alas, a few baby bluebirds.

Every late spring you turn up, regular
as birthdays. Another due, we wonder
who will attend. Will you, veteran of many
herpetological years in our wild yard?

And spiraling back upon myself, will I?

Another New Year's Morning

I know there will come a day
when you will be with me no more.
I would lure you with Turkish figs,
Grecian pomegranates, grapes from Provence,
Austrian chocolates filled with liqueur,
Chilean strawberries in champagne—
but by then you may no longer hunger.

So as New Year's Days replace
one another with startling cadence,
I cherish this morning, and arrange
blood oranges from Haifa, clementines
from Portugal, blueberries from Maine.
For now, you are here. We savor each
glistening sphere, sunrise-mirroring slice.

Trading in Essentials, November

"A torrent of shooting stars due tonight,
between two and four a.m., says Weather."
You close down your server for dinner.

Eleven p.m. bundled in coats, by flashlight
we dodge fallen trees as we walk to the dock.
Bright stars remain fixed in their heights.

Most birds gone in November. "A bummer,"
you shiver. "Get some sleep. I'll check my
                                        stocks."
We give up the night to the dark.

Insomnia hits me at two. Jacket tight
against cold, I navigate the yard blind,
lie back on the dock, study the sky.

How many around the earth wait years
for omens, signs, change (any way or kind),
birth, death, help in the dark, a star?

At last, through the Milky Way, one spark
seems to burn through space, disappears.
A heron croaks low, vanishes into black.

Nothing more. Freezing, I flee indoors.
Though awake until dawn, one meteor
and one bird are well worth the night.

Elisavietta Ritchie's poems, stories, creative non-fiction, journalism, photographs, and translations appear in numerous publications in the United States and abroad. *Tightening The Circle Over Eel Country* won the Great Lakes Colleges Association's "New Writer's Award;" *Raking The Snow* and *In Haste I Write You This Note: Stories & Half-Stories* were Washington Writers' Publishing House winners, and four stories were winners in the PEN/NEA Syndicated Fiction Project. "Camille Pissarro's *THE BATHER*" won *The Ledge* 2011 poetry prize. She received two Poetry Society of America annual awards and several Pushcart and other nominations.

Her publication credits include *The New York Times, Christian Science Monitor, Washington Post, National Geographic, JAMA: Journal of the American Medical Association, Poetry, The American Scholar, Nimrod, New Republic, Confrontation, Potomac Review, New York Quarterly, Bay Weekly,* and many others both literary and general. Anthologies with her work include *Sound and Sense* and *The 90th Anniversary Poetry Anthology*.

Several composers, including Jackson Berkey, David Owens, David L. Brunner, and others, have transformed her poems for voice and piano.

CPSIA information can be obtained at www.ICGtesting.com
Printed in the USA
LVOW11s1830300416

486104LV00001B/18/P